Sistrum

Flute and drum

Ruth

Cymbals

Assyrian harp

Goliath and David

A typical Mesopotamian building—a "Ziggurat"

Solomon

Dromedary

Saul

Assyrian chariot drawn by donkeys

Floor plan for the temple built by Solomon

Rooms

Ark

Lampstands

Bronze columns

Jonah

A trumpet made from an animal horn

Samson

Elijah

Daniel

Phoenician boat

A two-story Palestinian house. The lower level was used for animals.

Egyptian boat

Nihil Obstat: Rev. James M. Cafone, M.A., S.T.D., *Censor Librorum*
Imprimatur: ✠ Most Rev. John J. Myers, J.C.D., D.D., *Archbishop of Newark*

From an idea by Andrea Dami
ILLUSTRATED BY TONY WOLF
Original Italian text by Anna Casalis

© 2005 Dami International, Milano

Printed in China

English text © 2004 by Catholic Book Publishing Co.
77 West End Road, Totowa, NJ 07512
All rights reserved.

(T-835)

Illustrated by

TONY WOLF

THE ★ BIBLE ★

CATHOLIC BOOK PUBLISHING CO.
New Jersey

THE CREATION

In the beginning God created the heavens and the earth.
The FIRST day He separated the light from the darkness.
The SECOND day He created the firmament and He called it the heavens.

The THIRD day He commanded the earth to bring forth life, creating the plants with their fruit.

The FOURTH day He placed the sun, the moon and the stars in the heavens.

The FIFTH day He placed the fish in the seas and the birds in the sky.

The SIXTH day He filled the earth with animals of every species and He created humans in His image and likeness.
On the SEVENTH day He rested.

ADAM AND EVE

God created a small piece of Paradise, the Garden of Eden. He placed the first man there, Adam. God also created the first woman, Eve, so that Adam would not be alone. There was a large tree in the middle of the garden, which was filled with fruit. The Lord said, "You can eat any of the different types of fruit that you desire except for the fruit on that large tree, the tree of Good and Evil. Do not eat or you will die!"

Adam and Eve lived in peace and harmony. They did not wear any clothing, but they were not ashamed or embarrassed.

The serpent was the most clever of all the animals. One day it said to Eve, "Why don't you try those beautiful red apples that are growing on the tree of Good and Evil? You won't really die. You will actually become as powerful as God."

Eve trusted the serpent and ate some of the fruit. She then gave a bit to Adam. Suddenly they realized that they were naked, and they were ashamed. The Lord knew what they had done, and He was angry. "You have disobeyed Me, and you will be punished! From now on you will have to work to obtain your food from the land. You will be hungry and cold as well. And you, Eve, will suffer when you bring children into the world." He expelled them from the Garden of Eden.

CAIN AND ABEL

Expelled from Eden, Adam and Eve learned how to grow crops and how to hunt. They had two sons: Cain and Abel. Cain was a farmer and he offered some of his harvest to the Lord. Abel raised sheep and he offered the best from his flock to the Lord. The Lord was more pleased with Abel's sacrifice than Cain's. Cain became jealous of his brother.

The jealousy quickly became hate. One day he said to Abel, "Let's go out into the fields."

Abel did not suspect anything.

As soon as they were out of sight, Cain attacked and killed Abel, believing that no one had seen what he had done. But the Lord saw him and asked him, "Where is Abel?"

Cain boldly answered, "How should I know? Am I my brother's keeper?" The Lord punished Cain, condemning him to a life of flight and wandering.

Adam and Eve had another son, Seth. He was the founder of a race of people whom the Lord loved.

NOAH'S ARK

The descendants of Adam and Eve grew numerous. They soon became proud and did evil things. God, regretting having created them, decided to punish them. He wanted to save Noah, however, for Noah was wise, just and honest. God told Noah, "Build a large ark and take your wife and sons aboard. Choose a male and female from every land animal and every bird that flies in the sky and bring them into the ark so that they can one day resettle the earth. Store up an abundant supply of food. It is going to rain upon the earth for forty days and forty nights until everything is under water." Noah did all God had commanded him to do. It began to rain as God had said. Soon there was a great flood.

Every creature upon the earth died. The clouds then parted and a rainbow appeared in the sky.

Noah sent out a raven to see whether the water had receded, but everywhere it went it was still flooded. He then sent out a dove, but in vain. A week later, Noah sent out the dove again. This time the bird returned with an olive branch in its beak, a sign that the earth was blooming again and that God had finally made His peace with humanity.

THE TOWER OF BABEL

When the flood was over, the animals left the ark and repopulated the earth. The sons of Noah (Shem, Ham and Japheth) refounded the human race. People began to act and even look different from each other, but everyone still understood each other perfectly.

The descendants of Noah gathered and said, "Let us build a city. We will put a tower in its center to reach up into the heavens where God dwells."

The Lord was against this plan for He understood that they were doing this because of pride and not for love of Him. He frustrated their plans by confusing their language. The project, frustrated by a confusion of voices and languages, quickly ground to a halt. The tower of Babel was never finished. People were suddenly strangers to each other, and so they went their own ways, each nation traveling to its own land.

ABRAHAM AND ISAAC

The years went by. One of the descendants of Shem, Abraham, traveled with his family to live in the land of Ur. He heard God saying to him, "Abraham, depart from the land where you are now living and travel to a new land that I will show to you. You will be the father of a great people whom I will bless."

Abraham set out with his wife, Sarah, their friends and their families. They finally arrived in a land called Canaan. The Lord appeared to him and said, "Behold the land that I have promised to you and your descendants!"

Abraham built an altar there. He was very old and very tired from the journey. His wife was also very old and never had any children. Still, the Lord appeared to Abraham in a dream and told him that his descendants would be as numerous as the stars. How could this be possible?

Despite Abraham's age, he trusted in God. Sarah had a son whom they named Isaac, a handsome and strong boy. But the Lord tested Abraham's faith by saying to him, "Abraham, Abraham, take Isaac and go with him to a mountaintop. There you will sacrifice him to your Lord!"

Abraham, grief-stricken, took the boy and traveled to the mountain along with two donkeys that carried wood for the sacrifice. Abraham told Isaac to lie down upon the rocks. He then prepared to offer him in sacrifice.

Suddenly he heard a voice from the heavens that said, "Do not harm your son, Abraham! Now I know that you love Me; you are willing to sacrifice what is most dear to you! Return home with the boy and be blessed forevermore!"

Abraham looked up, saw a ram whose horns were caught in a bush, captured it and offered it up to the Lord in place of his son.

When Isaac was forty years old, he married Rebekah. She had twin sons, Esau and Jacob. When her sons were about to be born, the Lord said to Rebekah, "There are two sons in your womb. They will be rivals, and the older will serve the younger."

Esau, the firstborn, was a rugged hunter, but Jacob was a pale young man with a gentle heart. Esau loved the outdoors and went hunting with his father. Jacob, on the other hand, loved to stay at home with his mother. He was her favorite. One day, Esau returned from the hunt, dead tired. He saw Jacob sitting quietly in the tent before a steamy plate of lentils.

He said to his brother, "Give me some of those lentils. I am hungry."

Jacob answered, "I will give you some in return for your birthrights as the firstborn."

Esau accepted the trade. From then on, Jacob was considered to be the firstborn, giving him certain special rights. Isaac, having grown old, was all but blind. When he realized that he was about to die, he summoned his first-born son to give him his blessing. Jacob, aided by his mother, came to his father dressed like his brother. He thus received the blessing and his father's inheritance. This is how he fulfilled what God had foretold to Rebekah.

JOSEPH AND HIS BROTHERS

Jacob was now the head of the family, but he fled for fear of Esau's wrath. He met a beautiful young woman, Rachel, and he married her. Jacob had twelve sons, but he loved Joseph in a special way. Joseph was gentle and kind, and he had very unusual dreams.

One day he told his brothers, "I had a dream that I was in the fields tying together bunches of grain. While my bunch stood up straight, yours bowed down in front of mine."

The brothers became jealous and began to hate him.

Jacob even gave Joseph a beautiful, colored robe to show him how much he loved him.

Once the brothers were tending their flocks and Jacob said to Joseph, "Go see how the animals are doing, then come back home." The brothers simply decided to rid themselves of him.

The brothers tore off his robe and sold him to a passing caravan of Egyptian merchants. The brothers then returned to Jacob and showed him Joseph's robe, which they had dipped in a lamb's blood. They said, "Our poor brother has been killed by a wild animal." Jacob began to weep.

In the meantime, Joseph was led down to Egypt as a slave where an interesting new life awaited him.

Pharaoh, the high king of Egypt, had a strange dream one night. He dreamed that he was standing on the shores of the Nile River. He saw seven fat cows and then seven thin cows that ate the first cows. He had a similar dream about seven stalks of wheat. Pharaoh was disturbed and wanted to speak to someone who could interpret these dreams. Joseph was brought to Pharaoh and was told about the dreams.

He told him, "Your dreams, O king, indicate that Egypt will have seven years of plenty followed by seven years of famine. My advice is that you appoint someone to prepare for those difficult years."

Pharaoh immediately decreed, "You will be that person."

Joseph then began to collect a supply of grain so that no one in Egypt would suffer from hunger when the famine began.

The drought also affected Jacob's land. He told his sons, "Go to Egypt, where there is plenty; otherwise we will starve to death!"

Imagine the brothers' surprise when there they found their brother, whom they had betrayed and sold into slavery. Now he was famous and important. Joseph forgave his brothers and sent them back to bring Jacob to live with them in Egypt.

23

MOSES

After the death of Joseph, the twelve tribes of Israel, the descendants of the twelve sons of Jacob, had no one to defend them. They ended up as slaves. Pharaoh ordered that all the newborn Israelite boys be put to death in order to reduce the number of Israelites.

A woman from the tribe of Levi, who had just given birth to a baby boy, hoping to save him, placed him in a basket in the Nile River. Meanwhile, the daughter of Pharaoh was bathing a little downstream.

Seeing the baby in the basket, she said to her servant: "This must be an Israelite baby.

Quick, go look for a woman to nurse him." The mother of the abandoned baby presented herself to the princess and was told, "Nurse this baby for me." The princess continued, "I will pay you well. We will name him Moses, for that means, 'saved from the waters.'"

Moses' mother then raised him. Later, the princess had him educated as a prince in the royal palace. When older, he came to know about the terrible conditions in which the Israelites were living. Once he saw a soldier beating an Israelite slave. He became enraged, and he attacked and killed him. He fled to a distant land. There, God spoke to him saying, "Moses, lead My chosen people, the people of Israel, out of Egypt to the land of Canaan, the land flowing with milk and honey. Tell Pharaoh that if he does not listen to Me, I will come and perform wondrous deeds."

Moses returned to Egypt and asked Pharaoh to free his people, but he refused. The Lord grew angry and sent ten terrible plagues upon Egypt.

THE TEN PLAGUES

In the first plague, the waters of the Nile, the river that made Egypt fertile, turned into blood. But Pharaoh would not listen. Then millions of frogs came out of every pond, the river and every well in the land. They spread out and ruined the crops. Pharaoh was upset, and he promised to let the Israelites leave. But as soon as the frogs were gone, he took back his promise. Swarms of mosquitoes followed, then flies and gnats, and then there was a horrible outbreak of disease among the livestock.

The sixth plague afflicted humans. Tormented and weakened, the Egyptians became sick and were covered with sores and boils.

In the seventh plague, hail fell on the fields, sparing only the land of Goshen, where the tribes of Israel lived.

The eighth plague brought clouds of locusts that blocked out the sun and covered the land, devouring every remaining plant. But Pharaoh would not give in.

So God sent a ninth, terrible plague. The sun suddenly became black, leaving everything in darkness for the next three days.

Still, Pharaoh continued to prevent Moses and his people from leaving.

THE FLIGHT FROM EGYPT

And so the tenth plague, the most horrible, was proclaimed: All the firstborn of every family in Egypt would die. Moses ordered that all Israelites kill a lamb and mark their doors with its blood as a sign to the angel of death to pass over the Israelites when it did its terrible deed. They did this, and when the plague of death arrived that midnight, the firstborn of the Israelites were saved. But cries of grief rose from the houses of the Egyptians. Pharaoh did not have the courage to resist anymore. He summoned Moses and his brother Aaron. Broken and defeated, he said to them, "Go, leave us alone, you and your people!"

After 430 years of slavery, the people of Israel finally set out toward the Promised Land. They carried everything with them that they could gather together. The Israelites did not

know the paths through the desert that they were entering, and they were frightened that they might become lost. To guide them, the Lord assumed the form of a cloud by day and a column of fire by night.

Pharaoh quickly changed his mind about having let the Israelites leave because they were needed as slaves.

He cried out, "We will make them come back!"

He, together with six hundred chariots and thousands of warriors, set out in pursuit. They quickly found the signs left by the fleeing band, and they realized that they were heading toward the Red Sea.

They thought, "The Israelites made a mistake. Now we will trap them between the desert and the sea so that they cannot run away from us."

THE RED SEA

The fleeing Israelites quickly saw the army of Pharaoh approaching from a distance. They said to Moses, "Why did you bring us out here to be killed by the Egyptian cavalry in the desert?"

But the Lord spoke to Moses, telling him which way they should go. When they arrived on the shore of the Red Sea, Moses stretched out his arms over the water. The waves suddenly parted and a dry path appeared.

The Israelites marched out into the narrow path, sure that they would be protected by God. Pharaoh and his soldiers hurried after them. As soon as the Israelites reached the other shore, Moses stretched out his hands over the water a second time, and the waves crashed down upon the Egyptians, their chariots and their horsemen.

The Israelites, having seen the terrible destruction of the Egyptian army, followed Moses with renewed hope. But the way was long and difficult, and they quickly used all their supplies. The people complained, "It would have been better to remain as slaves in Egypt than to die of hunger and thirst in this desert!" But he told them to trust in the Lord's providence. That evening a large flock of quail landed near their camp. The Hebrews caught them, cooked them and ate them until they were full.

At dawn the next day there was a strange white powder covering the ground. The Israelites asked Moses, "What is it?" Moses answered, "It is the bread that the Lord sent us. Collect it and eat it!"

Every morning from that day on they found this wonderful food, called "manna." When they reached the desert of Rephidim, where there was not a drop of water, Moses struck a rock with his staff. A spring of fresh water came surging out of the rock, quenching the people's thirst.

The Ten Commandments

Three months after leaving Egypt, the Israelites reached the foot of Mount Sinai and camped there. Moses, Joshua and some others approached the mountain to climb it and draw near God. A cloud covered the mountain peak.

Amid thunder, lightning and a blast of trumpets, God was revealing the law to His people. Moses remained on the mountain for forty days and forty nights. God gave two stone tablets on which were written the commandments of the covenant with Israel.

While Moses spoke with God, the Israelites grew tired of waiting. They wondered whether their leader would return. They threatened Aaron saying, "Moses is not returning. His God no longer appears to us. Find us some other gods to guide us on our way!"

Aaron, frightened, had them bring him all the gold that they had. Melting it, he formed a calf out of it. The people immediately began to dance around it and pray to this golden idol. When Moses returned, he saw what had happened. Disappointed and enraged, he broke the tablets of the law, smashing them on the ground. He cried out, "What have you done? Do you want God to punish us?" Many of the Israelites repented, and they begged for forgiveness.

Moses returned to the mountain and received two new tablets from the Lord. He placed them in a wooden ark that had been covered with gold: the Ark of the Covenant.

The people continued on their journey to the Promised Land, carrying the Ark. On their way they defended themselves against their enemies. Finally, after many trials they came within sight of the land of Canaan.

The Ten Commandments

1. I, the Lord am your God. You shall not have other gods besides Me.
2. You shall not take the name of the Lord, your God, in vain.
3. Remember to keep holy the Sabbath day.
4. Honor your father and your mother.
5. You shall not kill.
6. You shall not commit adultery.
7. You shall not steal.
8. You shall not bear false witness against your neighbor.
9. You shall not covet your neighbor's wife.
10. You shall not covet anything that belongs to your neighbor.

33

CROSSING OVER THE JORDAN

The Promised Land now lay straight ahead. But who lived there? Would they welcome them, or would they be their enemies? Moses sent spies to check out the land. The Israelites became frightened and wanted to go no further. God grew angry with them and sent them back into the desert. They spent the next forty years there before seeing the Promised Land again. Moses was very old when God had him climb another mountain. There He showed him the land of Canaan saying, "This is your homeland, Moses, but you will not enter it because you will soon go home to your fathers."

Moses said, "Give another leader to your people, O Lord." The Lord chose Joshua, who was young, strong and courageous. Moses blessed his successor and all the tribes of Israel and then closed his eyes for the last time.

The Lord said, "It is time for you to cross the Jordan River. I will give you this land as your new homeland." Joshua ordered the priests to carry the Ark of the Covenant into the river, with all the people following close behind. When the priests entered the river, the waters dried up, leaving dry land for them to walk on. Joshua ordered twelve men, one from each of the twelve tribes of Israel, to gather rocks from the riverbed. They piled them in their camp in their new land as a memorial of the miracle of the Jordan River.

THE WALLS OF JERICHO

The people of Jericho defended themselves behind the high walls of their city as they prepared for battle with the Israelite invaders. Joshua realized that he would not be able to conquer Jericho without a great loss of life.

So the Lord told him, "Go around the walls of Jericho with all of your soldiers for six days in a row. On the seventh day, have each of the priests carry a trumpet as they process in front of the Ark of the Covenant. Have them walk around the walls six times. On the seventh trip around the walls, play the trumpets and have all the people shout as loudly as possible. The walls of the city will crumble to the ground."

Joshua summoned his officials and priests and ordered them to do exactly as God had commanded. For six days the army of Israel walked around the walls while the defenders of the city looked down without understanding what they were doing. On the seventh day they carried the gleaming Ark of the Covenant preceded by the priests

who played loudly on their trumpets. They went around the walls seven times. The defenders asked themselves, "What do these people want? Is this the way that these strange soldiers fight?" At last, Joshua ordered, "Shout out! Everybody shout out as loudly as you can!"

A huge shout rose, rolling up into the heavens. That tremendous noise shook the walls of Jericho. They broke apart and crumbled, crashing down upon the soldiers beneath. The city was defenseless, and the Israelites quickly took over the streets and the houses. This is how Joshua miraculously conquered Jericho. News of this great wonder spread throughout the land of Canaan, leaving Israel's enemies filled with respect and fear.

GIDEON

Even after the children of Israel finally conquered the Promised Land, they had to fight new enemies. Fierce Midianite warriors forced them into the hill country.

An angel of the Lord spoke to Gideon, a poor, courageous farmer. "You have been chosen to lead your people into battle. Hurry, gather a small group of brave men. Choose only the strongest and then lead them to a spring of water to drink. You will take with you only those who do not bend their knees to drink."

Gideon obeyed the angel and gathered together a small army of three hundred. They were few to fight a war, but the Lord was with them. Gideon approached the enemy camp. He ordered each soldier to take a trumpet, a torch and a pottery jar. "Put your torch into the jar so that the enemy cannot see us as we approach. When we near the camp, follow my example!"

The Israelites approached in silence. Suddenly, as they drew near to the enemy camp, Gideon took out his torch and broke the jar, sounding the trumpet loudly. Everyone did just as he had done. The sudden noise and lights terrified the enemy. They thought that they were facing a large force. As they fled, they were overtaken and killed. The victorious Israelites cried out that Gideon should become their king. He answered, "No, you have only one King, God!"

SAMSON

The Israelites were soon threatened by another violent and powerful people: the Philistines. Around this time, a barren Israelite woman had a dream in which an angel told her, "You will have a son who will free Israel from the Philistines. But woe to whoever would cut his hair."

The child whom she bore was named Samson. He became a giant of a man who quickly terrorized the Philistines. His long hair, the source of his tremendous strength, helped him defeat entire enemy armies. The Philistines tried a million different ways to capture him, but always in vain. Then, Samson fell in love with a beautiful but evil woman named Delilah. The Philistines convinced her to find out the secret of Samson's strength. One night, while he was peacefully asleep, she cut his hair. When he woke up, Samson found himself weak. The Philistines blinded him, bound him in chains and forced him to turn the wheel of a millstone.

They said, "Let's bring Samson inside. We'll have fun by making him dance around." They brought him into a great room, not realizing that his hair had again grown long. But Samson knew, for he had felt his strength return as his hair grew back.

During the feast, he asked God to help him. Samson then pushed on the columns of that room with all of his strength, crying out, "May Samson die with all of the Philistines!" The columns broke and the roof of the banquet room came crashing down, burying all of those present.

RUTH

The Bible speaks about things besides wars and violence and people having to flee. It also has many wonderful stories like that of Ruth, a young, gentle and beautiful widow. Her mother-in-law, Naomi, wanted to return to Bethlehem, her hometown, after her son's death. Ruth refused to abandon her; she accompanied her home. They were very poor. Ruth, to get a little food for herself and for Naomi, used to go to collect some grain that the harvesters had left in the fields after they had finished their work.

One day the owner of the field, a distant relative of Naomi named Boaz, heard Ruth's sad story. He told her, "Collect as much grain as you want. You can also draw water from my well. I have heard how well you have treated Naomi and how you left your homeland to help her."

So Ruth went each day to collect grain in the fields of Boaz, and they often met near the well. Boaz fell in love with her, and he wanted to marry her. But, according to tradition, it was Ehimelech, a man more closely related to Naomi than he, who had the right to marry Ruth. Since Ehimelech was already married, he gave to Boaz his rights to marry Ruth. The two young people married and were very happy.

Boaz and Ruth became the great-grandparents of a great king: David.

SAUL

The people of Israel needed someone who could lead them in God's ways. The Lord sent them Samuel, who for many years was their spiritual guide. He would communicate God's will to them. But the Israelites continually had war made against them, so they asked Samuel to "choose someone to be king for us to rule and protect us!"

While Samuel was meditating on how to do this, a handsome and strong young man appeared before him. He said, "You know everything! Tell me where I can find my father's donkeys." This young man was Saul. Samuel immediately understood that he had been sent by the Lord.

He told Saul, "Don't worry about your donkeys. Come with me; I will make you the king of Israel." The people were pleased with the choice, and they accepted Saul as their king.

Saul was courageous and a powerful fighter, but he had a bad personality and often gave foolish orders. During an especially dangerous battle against the Philistines, he commanded his men, "No one should eat anything until we win this war. Anyone who disobeys this command will be accursed."

But the men became hungry and grew too weak to fight. Jonathan, the courageous son of Saul, was in the woods with his soldiers and had not heard his father's command. He saw a honeycomb at the base of a tree and he ate it, and he immediately felt a surge of energy run through him.

One soldier said, "What have you done? You have disobeyed the king, and you will be punished." "My father made a mistake," Jonathan answered. "If we had all eaten well, we would have been stronger, and we would have defeated the Philistines without any difficulty." This was one example of how Saul was not a very good king.

DAVID AND GOLIATH

As the years passed by, Saul became more moody and arrogant. He often fought with Samuel who scolded him for not obeying the Lord. Samuel decided to search for a new king for Israel. One day he saw a handsome young shepherd in Bethlehem: David. The Lord told him, "Get up, Samuel, anoint this boy with holy oil. He will be the next king of my people." David came to the king's court to play the harp, and Saul loved him. He would always be comforted when depressed if David were around. But there always seemed to be another fight. The Philistines, led by a giant warrior named Goliath, were threatening their borders. No one had the courage to challenge him.

One day David said, "I cannot put up with the fact that this Philistine keeps insulting the people of Israel. I will go fight with him." Saul laughed while he answered, "But you are only a boy!" David answered confidently, "A boy? You'll see!"

Without wearing armor, he took a sling and six stones and boldly set out for the Philistine camp.

"What do you want, boy?" asked a shocked Goliath when he saw the boy approaching. Fearless David answered, "Fight me!" The giant approached him, carrying a lance. David simply twirled his sling and let loose a stone that struck Goliath right between the eyes. The giant dropped to the ground like a stone. When Saul died, David became king and was wise, religious and strong.

SOLOMON

When good King David was about to die, he summoned his favorite son, Solomon, and counseled him always to follow the Lord. Solomon was a just and merciful ruler.

One day two women came before him, bringing a baby with them. The first woman said, "He is my son!" "That's not true, he is mine! I want justice," said the second. To stop their fighting, wise Solomon proposed, "Let's cut the baby in two so that way each of you will have a half." "Don't kill him! I'd rather give up my rights to him," cried one of the women, showing Solomon who was the real mother.

Under strong and peaceful King Solomon, Israel reached the peak of its power. He decided to build a great temple in Jerusalem, Israel's most important city. For seven years, thousands of bricklayers, carpenters, woodworkers, sculptors and stonecutters worked to build it.

The finished temple was magnificent. The interior was covered with cedar wood from Lebanon, and the altar was made of purest gold. The Ark of the Covenant was placed inside of it.

ELIJAH

Not all of the kings of Israel were as wise as David and Solomon. In time an evil man, Ahab, became king. He married Jezebel, who was even worse than he was. The king and the queen abandoned the Lord and adored a false god named Baal. Many of their subjects followed their lead, and they began to worship idols.

Elijah, who had a solid faith and a courageous spirit, preached the word of the Lord, proclaiming disaster upon those who turned their backs upon the only true God. He often confronted the king, but always in vain. Finally, a great drought began in Israel. Elijah went to Ahab and his priests and challenged them: "Sacrifice an ox to your false idols. I will do the same on the Lord's altar. We will both pile up a mound of wood and see if Baal can set it on fire."

This is what they did. While Baal did not set fire to the wood, a huge fire erupted from the mound of wood that Elijah had prepared. Then, to extinguish the flames, a

50

downpour came from the heavens, ending the drought. Many of those who saw this wonder realized the error of their ways and changed. But Ahab and Jezebel continued in their wickedness and arrogance. Elijah, the prophet, predicted that they would meet a terrible end. Ahab was struck by an arrow, and Jezebel and her sons were also killed.

Elijah, however, did not die. When he was very old, the Lord told him to cross over the Jordan. A chariot came down in a whirlwind, and it carried him into heaven. God continued to send other prophets after Elijah to try to keep the people in the ways of the Lord.

JONAH

nother prophet of the Lord was Jonah, and he faced a great adventure. One day God asked him to go to the city of Nineveh. He was to preach to the sinful people there. Jonah was afraid to go to this great city. He did not think that he could do what God asked of him; he decided to board a ship and run away to sea.

The Lord sent a terrible storm with high waves that almost sank the boat. Each sailor prayed to his own god. Jonah, ignoring everything, slept. His terrified companions woke him up saying, "Who are you?" They asked, "Why does your God punish us so horribly?" Jonah told them why he deserved his Lord's anger. He begged the sailors to throw him into the waves in order to calm God's wrath. As the ship was about to sink, they threw Jonah into the waves. The sea immediately became calm. All there acknowledged God's power and thanked Him.

Jonah swam along until a huge fish swallowed him. Remaining in its belly for three days and three nights, he prayed to God the whole time and asked pardon. The fish brought him to shore, placing him on the beach.

Jonah went to Nineveh and preached there as the Lord had commanded him. Filled with fear, the people fasted and offered sacrifices to ask for pardon of their sins.

The city was thus saved from the Lord's anger, but Jonah was not happy. "Why did You forgive their faults so easily?" he asked. God explained that He loved and had mercy upon the people of that great city the same way people care for new plants to help them grow. Though weak and foolish, the people also were ready to repent and ask for forgiveness.

In Exile

The great king and lord of Babylon, Nebuchadnezzar, brought his army to the gates of Jerusalem. He had conquered many lands and peoples, and he wanted the kingdom of Israel as well.

The Israelites resisted for two years. Many of them tried to flee, but they were caught and killed. Jerusalem was eventually taken and burned to the ground. The great temple of Solomon crashed down upon the charred remains of its walls. Zedekiah, the Israelite king, and all the leading citizens were carried off as prisoners into Babylon.

The Israelites were forced to work as slaves in Nebuchadnezzar's court. But some of the young people were brought to the royal palace to learn the language and customs of the Babylonians. Among these were Daniel, Hananiah, Mishael and Azariah.

One night Nebuchadnezzar had a dream. A huge gold, silver, bronze and clay statue crashed to the ground, smashing into a million pieces. He asked Daniel, the wisest of the young Israelites, what this meant.

Daniel said, "The dream means that after you die, your kingdom will be broken up into smaller kingdoms." Impressed by this prediction, the king named Daniel an official in his kingdom. He also assigned the other three young men important responsibilities.

The Babylonians were pagans who worshiped a golden idol. One day the king had a large statue set up for all to worship. He ordered, "Whoever does not worship this golden statue will be thrown into a blazing hot furnace." The young Israelites said, "We have only one God and we cannot adore any other god." Nebuchadnezzar threw them into the furnace.

The young men walked around in the flames, but they were not harmed. Nebuchadnezzar recognized how powerful their God was and he freed them, permitting them to practice their own religion.

DANIEL

Balshazzar succeeded Nebuchadnezzar. He was a cruel king. One evening he held a great banquet, insisting that the cups that had been taken out of the temple in Jerusalem be brought to him. During the banquet, a great hand appeared and wrote the following words in the air with its fingers: *Mane, Tekel* and *Perez*. No one understood the meaning of these strange words.

Daniel was summoned and said to Balshazzar, "You have profaned the sacred cups of our God. You will be punished severely. *MANE* means that God has decided to put a quick end to your kingdom. *TEKEL* means that God has weighed you in a balance. *PEREZ* means that your kingdom will be divided between the Medes and the Persians."

That night Balshazzar was killed. Shortly afterward, the king of the Persians, Cyrus, conquered Babylon, entrusting its rule to Prince Darius. Darius, a wise and merciful prince, highly respected Daniel, whom he nominated as a governor of his kingdom.

Some officials, jealous of Daniel, said to the king, "Make a new law, O king, that people can pray and ask for things only from you. Whoever disobeys this command will be thrown into a lions' den." Darius followed their advice.

This was a trap designed to ensnare Daniel. The officials surprised him while he was praying to his God and reported it to the king. Darius, although he did not want to, observed the law and condemned Daniel. Before he had him thrown into the den, he said, "May your God save you."

That night the good king could not sleep, as he thought about Daniel and the lions. In the morning he ran to the den and cried out, "Daniel, Daniel, are you still alive?" Joyfully, Daniel answered, "I am alive, O king, for my God sent an angel who closed the jaws of the lions so that they could not harm me." The overjoyed king had Daniel set free, punished his enemies and restored all of Daniel's previous honors.

57

REBUILDING THE CITY

In time God inspired Cyrus, the great king of the Persians. He said, "The Lord of the heavens has granted me rule over all the kingdoms of the earth. He has ordered me to build a great temple in Jerusalem. All of its people can return to their homeland to rebuild the house of God. Those who cannot or do not want to return can help by donating whatever they can."

The Israelites started their trip back home. The kingdom of Israel no longer existed, and many foreigners were living in the Promised Land. Jerusalem had long been abandoned and destroyed. The Israelites began to rebuild their temple with enthusiasm. There were a thousand different opinions on how it should be done.

This was not a simple project. There were varied problems. Many were more concerned with building the city's walls and palaces than its temple in order to make it into a rich and powerful city. The Israelites were builders and defenders of their work all at the same time. The rebuilding went slowly, and the workers were weary. At last, King Darius, the successor of Cyrus, issued a law that no one should hinder their work.

Finally, after a long exile, the Israelites could celebrate the Passover, commemorating the "passing over" of the angel of death and the crossing of the Red Sea, in their rebuilt temple. It was not grand or covered with gold like that of Solomon, but the Israelites finally had a house in which they could honor their God.

Their God freed His people after centuries of wanderings and guided Moses in the exodus from Egypt, in the desert and across the sea. He guided Joshua in the conquest of the Promised Land and made Israel powerful during the reigns of Saul, David and Solomon. This was the God of Noah, Abraham, Jacob, the mighty Samson and the gentle Ruth.

The End

CONTENTS

CYPRUS

MEDITERRANEAN SEA

ALEXANDRIA

EGYPT

DESERT OF LIBYA

MEMPHIS

NILE RIVER

SINAI

RED SEA